WESTERN DANCING

Edward Murphy

Todd & Honeywell, Inc.
Great Neck, New York

Dedication
To my many friends who encouraged me to write these breakdowns, I dedicate this
book especially to Bob and Areline

Published by   Todd & Honeywell, Inc.
                      Ten Cuttermill Road
                      Great Neck, New York 11021

ISBN 0-89962-298-4

Manufactured in the United States of America.

Contents

PERSONAL QUOTES

Confucius once said *"A picture is worth a thousand words."*

Arthur Murray said *"Put fun in your life, try dancing."*

Now I say, *"Just remember you only have two feet so don't try to use anymore."*

Watching good dancers dance is half the fun. Learning how to dance is better.

Before you start following the SIMPLE INSTRUCTIONS for the Western Dances, it is beneficial to take advantage of learning Dance Terms before learning the SIMPLE BREAKDOWNS. We will explain in detail what they are and how they are to be used, as this will aid you in understanding the reason why you use certain movements with the music for each of the dances.

Learning the SIMPLE BREAKDOWNS for the Western Dances will give you a sense of achievement, doing them over and over again will give you confidence. We hope you will be pleased with your accomplishment.

Terms To Follow For Use In Western Dancing

BEAT — A HEAVY emphasis on the FIRST BEAT, ONE BEAT, DOWN BEAT or first HEAVY note in the music.

MELODY OF MUSIC — A soft and low beat in music.

TIME — There are two types of TIME used in dancing. They are (4/4) TIME and (3/4) TIME. This only means that the music was written so that the HEAVY BEAT of the music is heard on the FIRST BEAT.

Try to listen to a record and pick out the HEAVY BEAT in the music. You will notice that the HEAVY BEAT of music will reoccur on the FIRST BEAT if the music was written in (4/4) TIME or every FIRST BEAT of music if the music has been written in (3/4) TIME.

NOTE (4/4) TIME such as played in the following Western Dances. Cotton Eye Joe, Western Two Step, Houston Schottische, Four Corners you will

1

hear a HEAVY DOWN BEAT on the FIRST NOTE followed by two three four low NOTES and so on.

(3/4) TIME such as played in the following Western Waltz, Heel And Toe Polka and Put your Little Foot. You will hear a HEAVY DOWN BEAT on the ONE followed by two three and repeated by another One two three and so on, all through out the music.

TEMPO — This TERM refers to the orchestra leader, he sets the pace for the music and could play the piece either at a slow, medium or fast pace. Hence you have music in the same dance at a slow medium or fast speed.

BARS OF MUSIC AND INTRODUCTION — This TERM refers to the numbers of BEATS in a BAR of music. There are TWO BEATS in a BAR of music, if the music was written in (4/4) TIME or TWO BEATS in a BAR of music if the music was written in (3/4) TIME.

Again listen to a piece of music at the very beginning of a record and count how many BEATS there are before a HEAVY BEAT starts. You will notice that there will be either EIGHT FULL BARS of music, if the music is played in (4/4) TIME or again EIGHT FULL BARS of music, if the music is played in (3/4) TIME. This is called the INTRODUCTION PIECE. After the introduction has been played then the actual music will begin.   EXAMPLE

Now count the introduction as such:

in (4/4) TIME   1234 = 1 BAR
                 2234 = 2 BARS
                 3234 = 3 BARS
                 4234 = 4 BARS

now count the introduction as such:

in (3/4) TIME   123 = 1 BAR
                 223 = 2 BARS
                 323 = 3 BARS
                 423 = 4 BARS

until you have started into the actual down beat and melody of the music.

SLOW BEAT — A slow beat of music means that the dancer holds weight on one foot for two beats of music.

QUICK BEAT — A quick beat of music means the dancer holds weight on one foot for one beat of music.

This should begin to make sense to you when you start learning the SIM-PLE BREAKDOWNS of the dances.

CONTA CLOCK WISE — This TERM refers to the dance floor and the body alignments. A good dancer moves down the line of dance Conta Clock Wise around the dance floor.

2

MOVEMENT — This TERM we will use for learning these dances refers to the movements of the legs.

CHASSE — A chasse step consists of (3) three STEPS not patterns, STEPS in which the second Step comes together.

PATTERN — This TERM refers to a combination of steps put together forming a pattern.

FOOT WORK — This TERM refers to the actual placement of the feet.

ALIGNMENT — This TERM refers to the body and the movement of the body. It also refers to the direction in which the dancer should dance the patterns.

LINE OF DANCE — This TERM refers to how the dancer moves around the dance floor with his or her partner.

HOLD OF PARTNER — This TERM refers to the arms shoulders and body placement.

MEASURES OF MUSIC — We use this TERM in dancing for several reasons. The first reason we use a measure for in dancing is to complete a pattern, such as in a Waltz pattern. The second way that a measure is used for, is to be able to put several patterns together. Try to always count your measures when learning the patterns. This is very beneficial because you will be able to finish a pattern with the proper weight change of the feet.

EXAMPLE
Counting (8) measures in (4/4) time
1234 2234 3234 4234 5234 6234 7234 8234

Counting (4) measures in (3/4) time
1234 2234 3234 4234

Counting (8) measures in (3/4) time
123 223 323 423 523 623 723 823

Counting (4) measures in (3/4) time
123 223 323 423

SYMBOLS
(1) = weight change   (L.F.) = LEFT FOOT
(2) = weight change   (R.F.) = RIGHT FOOT
(3) = weight change

The SIMPLE BREAKDOWNS are EASY to master, it is in doing them over and over again until you can develop a smooth and comfortable movement practicing the patterns.

WESTERN WALTZ

MUSIC   Use Country Waltz Record
TIMING   3/4 TIME
TEMPOS   slow medium fast

We suggest using a slow Waltz record if you never danced a Waltz before as this will help you to change your weight properly.

FOOT WORK   MAN starts with the (L.F.)
                    LADY starts with the (R.F.)

HOLD OF PARTNER

Man places his left hand in the lady's right hand. Man puts right hand over lady's left shoulder. Lady places her right hand in the man's left hand, lady puts left hand around man's right shoulder.

TRAVELING STEP

MANS PART
Foward on the left foot (1)

Foward on the right foot passing the left foot (2)

Foward on the left foot (3) repeat the above movements for (8) measures

Note lady's part of traveling step for comment.

4

DIAGRAM

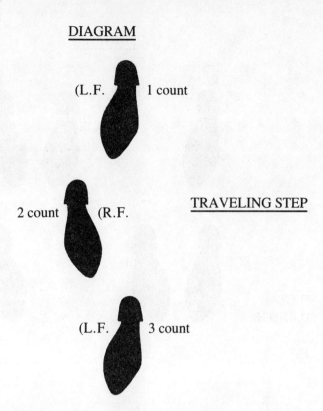

(L.F.   1 count

2 count   (R.F.   **TRAVELING STEP**

(L.F.   3 count

Note: Man's steps face down. Women's steps face up.

SQUARE STEP

MAN'S PART
Foward on the left foot (1)

Step to the right side with the right foot (2)

Bring the left foot to the right foot your feet should be together (3) now change weight (note this completes one measure and (1/2) square step

Back on the right foot (1)

Slide left with the left foot (2)

Bring right foot to left foot and change weight (3) (note this completes two measures and a full square step, it took two measures to complete a square step

DIAGRAM

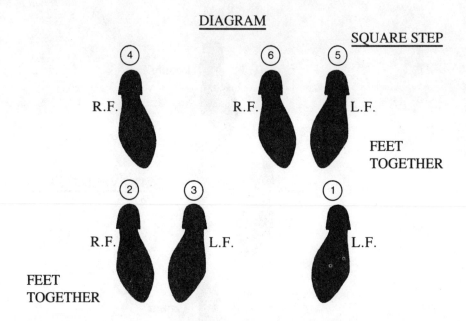

R.F.   R.F.   L.F.

FEET
TOGETHER

R.F.   L.F.   L.F.

FEET
TOGETHER

6

LADY'S PART
Back on the right foot (1)

Back on the left foot passing the right foot (2)

Back on the right foot passing the left foot (3) (note unless you use (8) measures to complete this pattern, you will not have the right foot free of weight and can not go into the square step so make sure you dance this pattern using eight measures

DIAGRAM

TRAVELING STEP

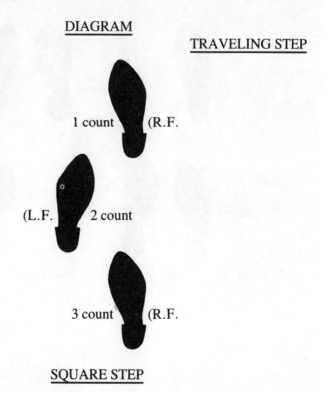

1 count   (R.F.

(L.F.   2 count

3 count   (R.F.

SQUARE STEP

LADY'S PART

Back on the right foot (1)

Step to the left side with the left foot (2)

Bring right foot to the left foot (3) your feet should be together, now change weight to left foot (note this completes one measure and (1/2) square step

Foward on the left foot (1)

Slide right with the right foot (2)

Bring the left foot to the right foot and change weight to left foot (3) note this completes two measures and a full square step, now notice it took two measures to complete a full square pattern.

DIAGRAM

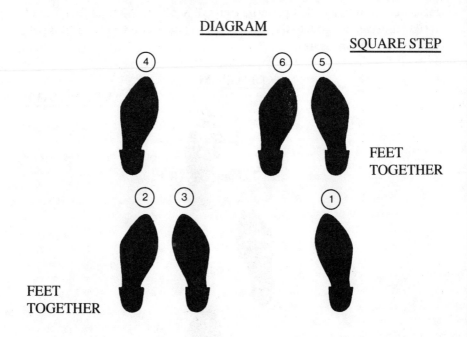

FEET
TOGETHER

FEET
TOGETHER

PUT YOUR LITTLE FOOT

<u>Music</u> — Use Put Your Little Foot Record
<u>Timing</u> — (3/4) Time
<u>Movement</u> — (38) Movements
<u>Tempo</u> — Slow to Medium

<u>NOTE</u> In this dance Put Your Little Foot, you will NOT put any weight on the FIRST BEAT or ONE BEAT, etc. (For example, listen to the words of Put Your Little Foot you will notice that the lyrics will tell you to put your little foot right out etc. But do NOT put weight on the words PUT, TAKE or OUT, as the pattern in this dance does not call for any weight on the first BEAT of the music. This will make sense to you when you study your breakdown.

There is no difference in the man's part or lady's part each start with the same foot. Man places lady to his right side and in front of him. Man puts his right arm around lady's shoulder placing his right hand into the lady's right hand. Man crosses his left arm in front of his chest and places his left hand into the lady's left hand.

CROSS STEP

<u>1st Movement</u> — Cross the left foot in front of the right leg no weight on the left foot (Notice no weight on the first beat). See diagram

9

<u>2nd Movement</u> — Bring left foot to the left side put weight on the left foot.

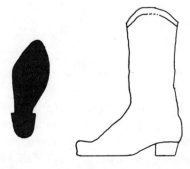

<u>3rd Movement</u> — Bring right foot to the left foot change weight to the right foot your feet should be together.

4th Movement — Cross the left foot in front of the right leg no weight on the left foot.

5th Movement — Bring left foot to the left side change weight to left foot.

6th Movement — Bring right foot to the left foot change weight to right foot your feet should be together.

7th Movement — Cross left foot in front of the right leg no weight on the left foot.

8th Movement — Bring left foot to the left side change weight to left foot.

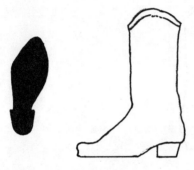

9th Movement — Cross right foot in front of left leg change weight on right foot.

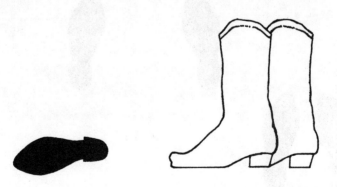

10th Movement — Bring left foot to the left side change weight to the left foot.

11th Movement — Right heel should be placed on the floor no weight on right heel.

12th Movement — Cross right foot in front of left leg no weight on right foot.

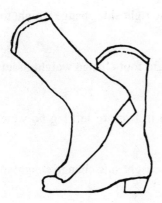

13

13th Movement — Bring right foot to the right side change weight to right foot.

14th Movement — Bring left foot to the right foot change weight to left foot your feet should be together.

The diagrams for right movements (Movements 15-22) are exactly the same as the left movements except that you travel to the right.

15th Movement — Cross right foot in front of left foot no weight on right foot.

16th Movement — Bring right foot to the right side change weight to right foot.

17th Movement — Bring left foot to right foot change weight to left foot your feet should be together.

18th Movement — Cross the right foot in front of left leg no weight on right foot.

19th Movement — Bring right foot to the right side change weight to right foot.

14

20th Movement — Cross left foot in front of right foot put weight on left foot.

21st Movement — Bring right foot to right side change weight to right foot.

22nd Movement — Left heel should be placed on the floor no weight on left heel.

The following movements are a repeat from the first step to the twenty second step

1st Movement — Cross the left foot in front of the right leg no weight on the left foot.

2nd Movement — Bring left foot to the left side put weight on left foot.

3rd Movement — Bring right foot to the left foot change weight your feet should be together.

4th Movement — Cross the left foot in front of the right leg no weight on the left foot.

5th Movement — Bring left foot to the left side change weight to left foot.

6th Movement — Bring right foot to the left foot change weight your feet should be together.

7th Movement — Cross left foot in front of right leg no weight on left foot.

8th Movement — Bring left foot to the left side change weight to left foot.

9th Movement — Cross right foot in front of left leg change weight on the right foot.

10th Movement — Bring left foot to the left side change weight to left foot.

11th Movement — Right heel should be placed on the floor no weight on right heel.

<u>12th Movement</u> — Cross right foot in front of left leg no weight on right foot.

<u>13th Movement</u> — Bring right foot to the right side change weight to right foot.

<u>14th Movement</u> — Bring left foot to the right foot change weight on left foot your feet should be together.

<u>15th Movement</u> — Cross right foot in front of left foot no weight on right foot.

<u>16th Movement</u> — Bring right foot to the right side change weight to right foot.

<u>17th Movement</u> — Bring left foot to right foot change weight to left foot your feet should be together.

<u>18th Movement</u> — Cross the right foot in front of left leg no weight on right foot.

<u>19th Movement</u> — Bring right foot to the right side change weight to right foot.

<u>20th Movement</u> — Cross left foot in front of right foot put weight on left foot.

<u>21st Movement</u> — Bring right foot to the right side change weight to right foot.

<u>22nd Movement</u> — Left heel should be placed on the floor no weight on left heel.

<u>23rd Movement</u> — Cross the left foot in front of the right leg no weight change. (See 7th Movement - page 12 - for diagram)

<u>24th Movement</u> — Bring left foot to the left side change weight to left foot. (See 8th Movement - p. 12)

<u>25th Movement</u> — Cross the right foot in front of left leg change weight on right foot. (See 9th Movement - p. 12)

26th Movement — Bring left foot to the left side right heel should be placed on the floor no weight on the right heel.

(See 10th, 11th Movements - p. 13)

27th Movement — Cross right foot in front of left leg no weight on right foot. (See 12th Movement - p. 13)

28th Movement — Bring right foot to the right side change weight on right foot. (See 13th Movement - p. 14)

29th Movement — Cross the left foot in front of the right leg change weight on left foot.

30th Movement — Bring right foot to the right side change weight to right foot. (See 19th Movement)

31st Movement — Cross the left foot in front of the right leg no weight on left foot. (See 7th Movement - p. 12)

32nd Movement — Bring left leg to the left side change weight to left foot. (See 8th Movement - p. 12)

33rd Movement — Cross the right foot in front of the left leg put weight on right foot. (See 9th Movement - p. 12)

34th Movement — Bring left foot to the left side change weight to left foot (right heel is placed on the floor no weight on right heel.)

(See 10th, 11th Movements - p. 13)

35th Movement — Cross the right foot in front of the left leg no weight on right foot. (See 12th Movement - p. 13)

36th Movement — Bring the right foot to the right side put weight on right foot. (See 13th Movement - p. 14)

37th Movement — Cross left foot in front of right leg change weight on left foot.

38th Movement — Bring right foot to the right side change weight to right foot left heel should be on the floor no weight on the left heel.

You may use a HOP on the right foot when crossing the left foot in front of the right leg.

17

WESTERN TWO STEP
"Oh The Fun Of It All"

MUSIC   Country Western Two Step music
TIMING   (4/4) TIME
TEMPO   Slow Medium Fast
BEATS   Slows and Quicks

It is always better to learn this dance with a slow tempo, however this dance (TWO STEP) should be danced in a medium to fast tempo, traveling conta clock wise around the dance floor.

HOLD OF PARTNER Man places left arm over lady's right shoulder and puts his right arm around lady's left shoulder. Lady places her right arm around man's left shoulder and puts her left arm on man's right hip.

TWO STEP

MAN'S PART

Forward on the left foot slow count (hold for two beats of music)

Forward on the right foot passing the left foot slow count (Hold for two beats of music)

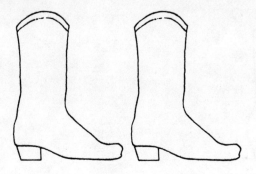

Forward on the left foot quick count (Hold for one beat of music)

Bring the right foot to the left foot put weight on the right foot for a quick count your feet should be slightly together left foot should be forward

LADY'S PART

Back on the right foot (Hold for two beats of music) slow count

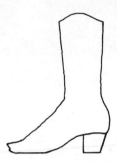

Back on the left foot passing the rignt foot (Hold for two beats of music) slow count

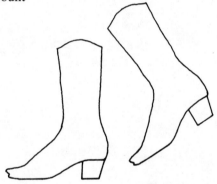

Back on the right foot (Hold for one beat of music) quick count

Bring left foot to the right foot (Hold for one beat of music) quick count

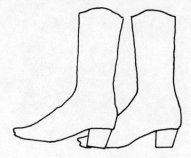

Your feet should be slightly together and your left foot should be forward

COTTON EYE JOE

MUSIC   Cotton Eye Joe record only
TIMING   (4/4) TIME
TEMPO   Slow Medium Fast
MEASURES   Four to Eight measures of music

We suggest using a slow TEMPO record to start with as it will help you to change your weight properly. There is no difference in the MAN'S PART or LADY'S PART each start with the same foot. Man places lady to his right and puts his right arm around LADY'S shoulder placing his right hand into the lady's right hand, man crosses his left arm in front of his chest and places his left hand into the lady's left hand.

STEP ONE

Left kick (a)
Commence kicking forward with the left foot twice before changing weight counting one, two

CHANGE STEP

Now change weight by placing left foot to the floor (1) shift your weight to your right foot (2) and back to the left foot (3) your right foot should be free of weight

STEP TWO

Right kicks (b)

Commence kicking forward with the right foot twice before changing weight counting one two

CHANGE STEP

Now change weight by placing your right foot to the floor (1) shift your weight to the left foot (2) and back to your right foot (3)

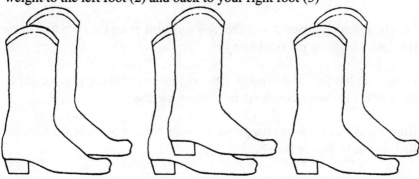

Left kick (a)
Commence kicking forward with the left foot twice before changing weight counting one two

CHANGE STEP

Now change weight by placing your right foot to the floor (1) shift your weight to the left foot (2) and back to your right foot (3)

Commence kicking forward with the right foot twice before changing weight counting one two your left foot should be free of weight.

CHASSE STEP

Start by reaching forward with the left foot now place the left foot to the floor (1)

Bring your right foot to the instep of the left foot now change weight (2) your feet should be slightly together

Now bring your left foot forward and put your weight on the left foot (3) your right foot should be free of weight

Start by reaching forward with the right foot now place the right foot to the floor put weight on the right foot (1)

Bring your left foot to the instep of the right foot and place your weight on the left foot (2) your feet shoud be slightly together

Bring right foot forward change your weight to the right foot (3) your left foot should be free of weight

24

Repeat the chasse movements for eight measures traveling down the line of dance conta clock wise around the dance floor counting your measures as such:123 223 323 423 523 623 723 823

Now go back to the beginning of the kick step (a) and start all over again

HEEL AND TOE POLKA

MUSIC	Any Country Polka Record
TIMING	(3/4) TIME
TEMPO	Medium to Fast
MEASURES	(4) measures
MOVEMENTS	(8) Movements

We suggest using a medium tempo record to start with as it will help you to change your weight properly. There is no difference in the man's part or lady's part, each start with the same foot. Man places lady to his right side and puts his right arm around lady's shoulder placing his right hand into the lady's right hand. Man crosses his left arm in front of his chest and places his hand into the lady's left hand.

1st Movement — Place your left heel forward to the floor leaving the weight on the right foot.

2nd Movement — Bring the left foot back to the right foot now change weight to the left foot your feet should be together.

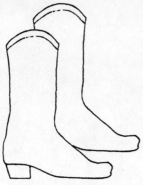

3rd Movement — Bring your right toe back touching the floor leaving the weight on the left foot.

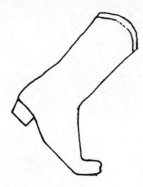

4th Movement — Place the ball of the right foot on the floor now passing the left foot bring ball on right foot forward without changing weight and kick forward.

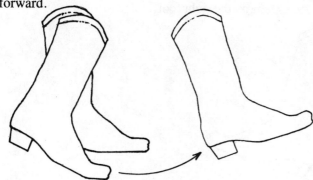

<u>5th Movement</u> — Now touch the floor with the right heel.

<u>6th Movement</u> — Bring the right foot back to the left foot your feet should be together change weight to the right foot.

<u>7th Movement</u> — Bring the left heel forward and place the left heel to the floor leaving the weight on the right foot.

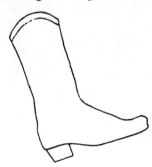

8th Movement — Bring left leg across and in front of the right leg your left foot should be free of weight and crossed in front of the right knee.

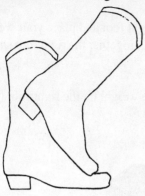

CHASSE STEP

Start by reaching forward with the left foot and place the left foot to the floor (1)

Bring your right foot to the instep of the left foot now change weight to the right foot (2) your feet should be slightly together the left foot should be slightly forward

Now bring your left foot forward and put your weight on the left foot (3) your right foot should be free of weight

Start by reaching forward with the right foot now place the right foot to the floor put weight on the right foot (1)

Bring your left foot to the instep of the right foot and place your weight on the left foot (2) your feet should be slightly together the right foot should be slightly forward

Bring your right foot forward placing the weight on the right foot (3) your left foot should be free of weight

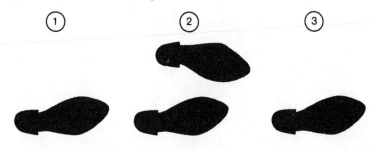

Now repeat the chasse movements for four measures traveling conta clock wise around the dance floor, making sure you count your four measures as follows 123 223 323 423
Now go back and repeat the heel and toes steps.

THE PUDDLE JUMPER
OR
COW CHIP DANCER

30

THE KICKER DANCER

ROBOT CHARLIES

STIFF STIFF STIFF

*THE WATER PUMP
DANCER*

31

FOUR CORNERS

MUSIC   Use any swing record
TIMING   (4/4) TIME
MEASURES   Eight measures of music
MOVEMENTS   Movements
TEMPO   Slow, Medium, Fast

We suggest using a slow tempo record to start with as it will help you to change your weight properly. There is no difference in the Man's Part or Lady's Part each start with the same foot. There is no holding of partners in this dance, each person does the FOUR CORNERS by themselves.

Before we begin four corners imagine yourself standing in the middle of a room. If you will notice the room will have four walls. We will call them corners in order to show you how to follow the directions for this dance. Each corner will be one quarter in width making a total of four quarter, or four corners.

DIRECTION OF THE BODY — While standing in the middle of the room face one wall, now turn 1/4 turn to the left this is the first corner. Turn 1/4 turn to the left again, this is the second corner turn 1/2 turn to the left this is the third corner and 1/2 turn to the left again, this is the fourth corner. You should be back to where you first started.

There are several variations for this pattern. However we will use the very basic movements in order for you to understand the breakdown.

There are sixteen movements to cover the four corners.

<u>1st Movement</u> — First corner kick forward with left foot no weight on left foot.

L.F.

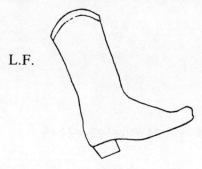

<u>2nd Movement</u> — Bring left foot back to right foot and change weight to left foot.

R.F.   L.F.

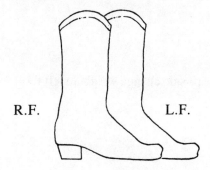

<u>3rd Movement</u> — Kick forward with right foot no weight on right foot.

R.F.

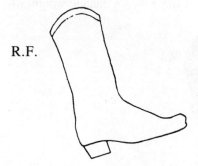

4th Movement — Bring right foot back to left foot change weight to right foot.

L.F.   R.F.

5th Movement — Kick forward with left foot no weight on left foot.

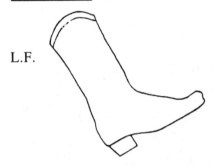

L.F.

6th Movement — Bring left foot to the left side change weight to left foot.

L.F.

LEFT
SIDE

7th Movement — Bring right foot back of the left foot change weight to right foot.

L.F.   R.F.

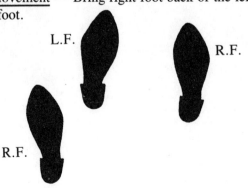

R.F.

34

<u>8th Movement</u> — Bring left foot to the left side change weight to left foot.

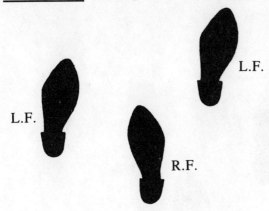

<u>9th Movement</u> — Kick forward with right foot no weight on right foot.

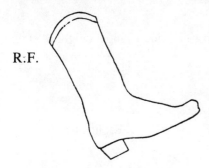

<u>10th Movement</u> — Bring right foot to the right side change weight to right foot.

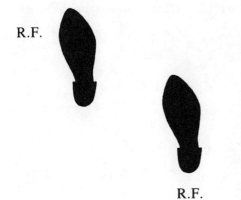

11th Movement — Bring left foot back of right foot change weight to left foot.

L.F.

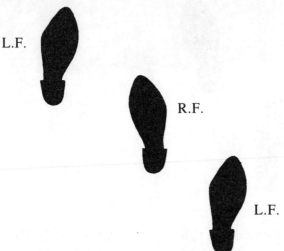

R.F.

L.F.

12th Movement — Bring right foot to right side change weight to right foot.

R.F.

 R.F.   Right side

13th Movement — Kick forward with the left foot no weight on the left foot.

L.F.

<u>14th Movement</u> — Leave left foot forward now put weight on left foot.

L.F.

<u>15th Movement</u> — Place weight back on right foot left foot should be in front of right foot no weight on left foot.

R.F.

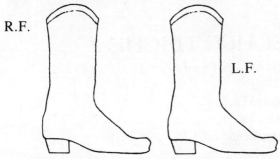

L.F.

<u>16th Movement</u> — Put weight on ball of left foot turning the body at the same time 1/4 turn to the left bring right foot around and in front of left foot put weight on right foot. You will notice that your body has changed to the second corner. Put weight back on left foot shift weight to right foot, your right foot should be forward.

L.F.

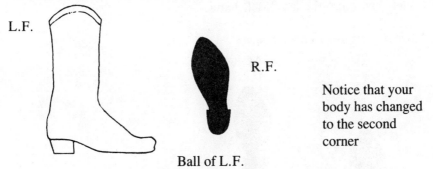

R.F.

Notice that your body has changed to the second corner

Ball of L.F.

FIRST CORNER GOING INTO THE SECOND CORNER
Now repeat first movement facing the second corner and so on until you have completed all four corners.

HOUSTON SCHOTTISCHE

<u>MUSIC</u>	Any Schottische Record
<u>TIME</u>	(4/4) TIME
<u>TEMPO</u>	Medium to Fast
<u>MEASURES</u>	(4) measures
<u>MOVEMENTS</u>	(4) Movements

We suggest using medium tempo of music to start with as it will help you to change your weight properly. There is no difference in the Man's or Lady's part each start with the same foot. Man places lady to his right side and puts his right arm around lady's shoulder placing his right hand into the lady's right hand. Man crosses his left arm in front of his chest and places his left hand into the lady's left hand.

Place the left foot to the left side

DIAGRAM 1

(LF)

1 Count

Left Side

Cross the right foot in back of the left foot change weight to right foot

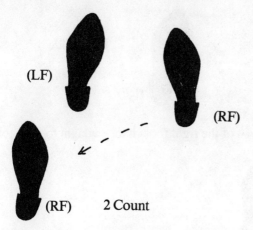

(LF)

(RF)

(RF)   2 Count

Bring left foot to the left side change weight to left foot

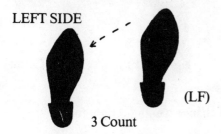

LEFT SIDE

(LF)

3 Count

Now kick the right leg across and in front of the left leg. No weight on right leg.

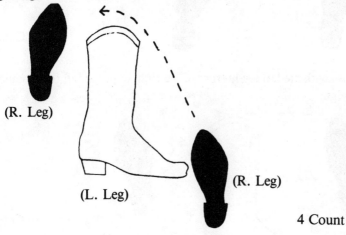

(R. Leg)

(L. Leg)

(R. Leg)

4 Count

Place the right foot to the right side change weight to right foot

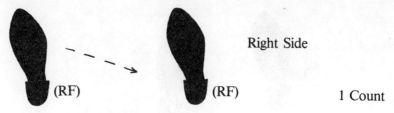

Right Side

(RF)   (RF)   1 Count

Bring the left foot in back of the right foot change weight to left foot

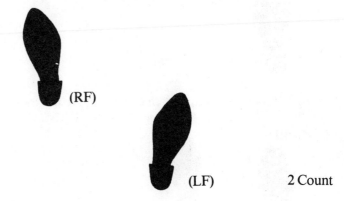

(RF)

(LF)   2 Count

Bring the right foot to the right side change weight to right foot

RIGHT SIDE

(RF)   3 Count

Kick across with the left leg in front of the right leg your left foot should be free of weight

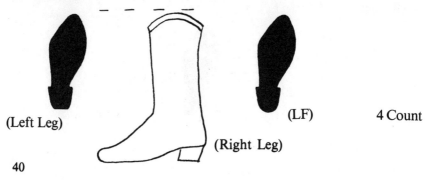

(Left Leg)   (LF)   4 Count

(Right Leg)

KICK STEP

Step forward with the left foot

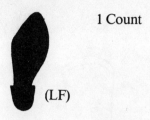

1 Count

(LF)

Kick across and in front of the left leg with the right foot

2 Count

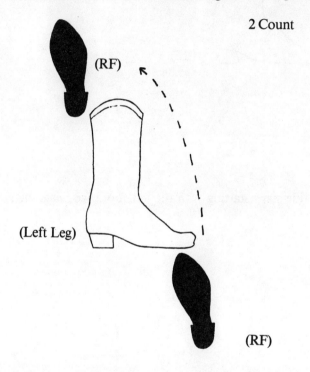

(RF)

(Left Leg)

(RF)

Step forward with the right foot

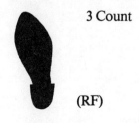

3 Count

(RF)

Kick across and in front of the right foot with the left leg

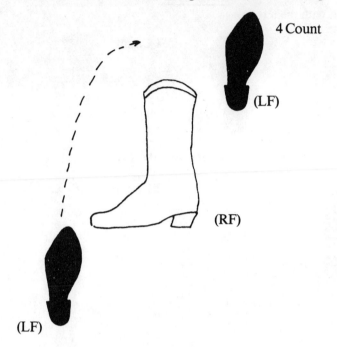

4 Count

(LF)

(RF)

(LF)

Now repeat the side steps starting with the left foot. See Diagram 1.